Let's Explore

Time

by Henry Pluckrose

W

FRANKLIN WATTS

NEW YORK • LONDON • SYDNEY

Author's note

This book is one of a series which has been designed to encourage young readers to think about the everyday concepts that form part of their world. The text and photographs complement each other, and both elements combine to provide starting points for discussion. Although each book is complete in itself, each title links closely with others in the set, so presenting an ideal platform for learning.

I have consciously avoided 'writing down' to my readers. Young children like to know the 'real' words for things, and are better able to express themselves when they can use correct terms with confidence.

Young children learn from the experiences they share with adults around them. The child offers his or her ideas which are then developed and extended through the adult. The books in this series are a means for the child and adult to share informal talk, photographs and text, and the ideas which accompany them.

One particular element merits comment. Information books are also reading books. Like a successful story book, an effective information book will be turned to again and again. As children develop, their appreciation of the significance of fact develops too. The young child who asks 'Why do we need clocks?' may subsequently and more provocatively ask, 'Who invented time?' Thoughts take time to generate. Hopefully books like those in this series provide the momentum for this.

Henry Pluckrose

Contents

Time is the word we use
to describe the space between
one moment and the next.
What words do you use
when you talk about time?

Once there was no you.
You had not been born.
But time still existed then.
Your mother and father
lived in this time.

This is a statue of
Florence Nightingale.
Florence was a famous nurse
who died almost 100 years ago.
She lived long before your
grandparents were born.

In the distant past, long before
there were any people at all,
great dinosaurs walked the earth.
You can see models of them
in museums.

At daybreak the sun rises.
At nightfall the sun sets.
The change from day to night
shows us that time has passed.

The seasons also show us
that time has passed.
Spring turns to summer,
autumn turns to winter.
What season of the year is it now?

Sometimes we need to
describe time exactly.
If everybody came to school
when they woke up in the morning,
everybody would arrive
at a different time!

We use clocks and watches
to tell us what time it is.
This clock has an hour hand
and a minute hand.
What time does the clock show?

The numbers on this digital clock show hours and minutes, too.

What other sorts of clocks
can you think of?

Being able to measure time means we can have timetables for buses, trains and aeroplanes.

We can also measure
periods of time.
How many hours,
minutes and seconds
did it take for this athlete
to run the marathon?

Time is also measured
in days, weeks, months and years.
We use calendars and diaries
to help us to do this.
Each day has a different date.
What is the date of your birthday?

10 years make a decade.

100 years make a century.

1000 years make a millennium.

The year 2000 was the start
of a new millennium.

There were special celebrations
all over the world.

Index

First published in 2000 by
Franklin Watts
96 Leonard Street
London
EC2A 4XD

Franklin Watts Australia
14 Mars Road
Lane Cove
NSW 2066

Copyright © Franklin Watts 2000

ISBN 0 7496 3657 2

Dewey Decimal
Classification Number 529

A CIP catalogue record for this book is
available from the British Library

Series editor: Louise John
Series designer: Jason Anscomb

Printed in Hong Kong

Picture Credits:
Steve Shott Photography, cover page, pp. 4,
28; Ray Moller Photography, title page, pp.
20, 23, 26; Alexander McIntyre pp. 6, 9;
Science Photo Library p. 12 (Nasa); Robert
Harding pp. 15 (D. Jacobs), 17 (A. Williams);
Eye Ubiquitous pp. 19 (Paul Seheult), 27
(Sean Aidan), 31 (Julie Mowbray); NHPA
p. 10 (Robert Erwin); Chris Fairclough
Photography p.25.
With thanks to our models:
Mamadu Tyson, José Ballesteros.